ZOOMABABY
and the Locked Cage

written by Michael Rosen
illustrated by Caroline Holden

Everything's quiet. It's the middle of the night. Everyone is asleep.

Even Ricky the Rat.

It was the warning signal on Pip's rattle.

But he doesn't hear it because he's fast asleep.

Someone needs help, but Pip sleeps on.

Jumbo the hamster wakes up and the moment she wakes up she jumps on to her wheel and starts running.

WHIRR! WHIRR! WHIRR!

Maybe this will wake Pip up!

No.

But it does wake up Ricky. When Ricky wakes up he starts burrowing down into his heap of wood shavings.

So now there's a Beep! Beep! from the rattle, Whirr-Whirr from the wheel and the Scrunch-Scurry from the shavings... and... and Pip wakes up.

And just like that, Zoomababy flapped his arms and flew out of his cot, out through the window and up into the air.

Up in the sky, Zoomababy could look down on the town.

Fatchops was in his pen, fast asleep.

The monkeys seemed happy enough. No snake in sight.

The wolves weren't howling. They were quietly grumbling, but not enough to wake the neighbours.

Where was Zack?

"I hope I'm not too late. What if Zack's been eaten alive by Twizzle the tiger?"

Then, suddenly, Zoomababy caught sight of a torch light. He whipped out his ⭐⭐ ZOOMAGLASSES ⭐⭐ Oh no! Zack was stuck in one of the cages.

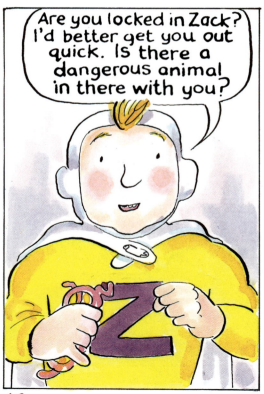

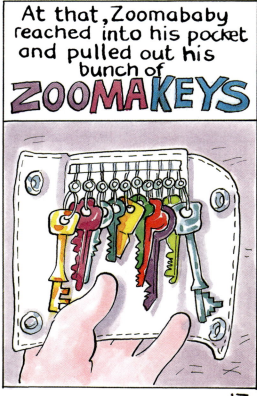

Back at the house Mum was still thinking...

"Yes, I'd better get up and check on him."

Out of the bed, on with the dressing gown.

At the zoo, something strange was happening. Zoomababy had opened the door of the cage but Zack wouldn't come out.

19

Mum was now out of the room and walking towards Pip's room.

"Oooh, I hope he's alright"

"You know how it is, Zack."

"If a job's worth doing, it's a job for ZOOMABABY!"

And up into the sky he zoomed, up over Sunnyside Zoo and back towards Story Street.

The lights were glowing and one quick peek through the zoomaglasses showed Zoomababy that there was a light on in his house.

I must get back in time.

Mum had just got to Pip's door.

She put her ear to the door.

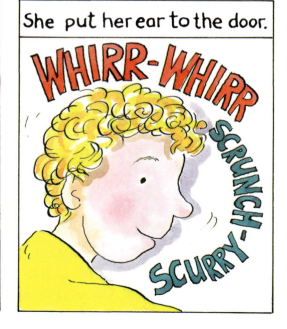

WHIRR-WHIRR SCRUNCH-SCURRY-

In through the window flew Zoomababy and landed in his cot, just as Mum was opening the door.